THE… …TEE

THE INFINITE GUARANTEE

A Meditation on the Last Words from the Cross

Andrew Cruickshank

Lakeland

LAKELAND
BLUNDELL HOUSE
GOODWOOD ROAD
LONDON S.E.14

ISBN 0 551 00109 7

Printed by C. Tinling & Co. Ltd., London and Prescot

CONTENTS

INTRODUCTION 7
FOREGROUND 9
INVOCATION 10
THE FIRST WORD: Father, forgive them; they do not know what they are doing 13
THE SECOND WORD: I tell you this: today you shall be with me in Paradise 25
THE THIRD WORD: Woman, behold thy son! Behold thy mother 35
THE FOURTH WORD: I thirst 47
THE FIFTH WORD: My God, my God, why hast thou forsaken me? 59
THE SIXTH WORD: Father, into thy hands I commit my spirit 77
THE SEVENTH WORD: It is finished 87

The Bible quotations in this volume are taken from various translations as follows:

The Authorized Version
The New English Bible
The New American Standard Bible
The New Testament, A New Translation (Moffatt)
The New Testament in Modern Speech (Weymouth)

Quotations from Søren Kierkegaard are drawn from *Training in Christianity* by Walter Lowrie, Princeton University Press and used by kind permission of the publishers.

For Curigwen and Ivor

INTRODUCTION

THE first time I was invited to meditate on the last words from the Cross in the three hours' service on Good Friday, it was a profound experience which left me drained of all interest, and I felt something of that dark night of total personal inadequacy. The second time, some years later, was not so painful. It was time to stop meditating and place the words on record for those whom it might interest.

It might interest those who, like me, believe that with the collapse of the classical world and Christendom the revelation of the Evangelists must be rediscovered as freshly as it came to those in Jerusalem at Pentecost. Indeed, if this rediscovery were not a continuing element in Christianity its credibility as the revelation of a creative God would be suspect. Within the last fifty years we have come to ask not merely what the New Testament is about, but how its revelation was vouchsafed.

For centuries we have accepted the canon fixed by the Early Christian fathers, first presented by Athanasius in the fourth century, when the dominant intention was to find a universality within the Gospels coherent with Greek thought, and the total interdependence of Church and state. Now that the Christian community has been fractured into its smallest member, the individual, the time has come to look again at the chronology of the revelation and ponder the consequences—for instance, the significance of the fact that Paul completed his letters before the evangelists composed the life. Did Paul know the last words? Or did he accept them as part of the early oral tradition of the Church that God made Christ the cursed one for us? Behind this meditation on the last words is the belief that the evangelists are composing an evolving pattern for individual behaviour consistent with the reality and truth of the world about us. The Christian insight must always be partial and expressed as a movement towards the rational. There is no finality here, but one man's view of the consequences for him of the last words from the cross.

For those who wish to reflect between the words I have included for guidance selections from a work of Søren Kierkegaard, who deemed that there was a need for training in Christianity in order to be contemporary with Christ.

FOREGROUND

THE man Jesus was born about the year 5 BC. At the age of one he was presented to the Lord in the Jewish Temple.

He began his teaching about the year 26, when he was thirty.

After two years the Sanhedrin, the governing body of the priestly state of the Jews, was persuaded that his teaching was blasphemous. Like Socrates, his teaching was considered corrupting, but whereas Socrates thought that the highest relationship was that between man and man, Jesus taught that it lay between man and God, a thing which was deeply offensive to the Covenant of Israel.

Less than a week before his arrest his triumphal entry into Jerusalem convinced the high priests of his threat to the state. After a last supper with his disciples he withdrew to the garden of Gethsemane to pray for assurance of his insight and purpose. It was in the garden that he was apprehended by the Jewish police, informed by Judas Iscariot, one of his disciples.

He was turned over to Pontius Pilate, the Roman governor of Palestine, who unwillingly condemned him to to be crucified. On the cross he was crowned with thorns and over his head a notice read THIS IS THE KING OF THE JEWS.

INVOCATION

It is eighteen hundred years and more since Jesus Christ walked here on earth. But this is not an event like other events, which, only when they are bygone pass over into history, and then, as events long bygone, pass over into forgetfulness. No, His presence here in earth never becomes a bygone event, and never becomes more and more bygone—as long as faith is to be found on earth. And if it is not, then indeed at that very instant, it is a long, long time since He died. But so long as there is one believer, such a one must, in order to become such, have been, and as a believer continue to be, just as contemporary with His presence on earth as were those first contemporaries. This contemporaneousness is the condition of faith, and more closely defined it is faith.

SØREN KIERKEGAARD

THE FIRST WORD

Father, forgive them; they do not know what they are doing.

Luke 23: 34

IN the twenty-third chapter of the third Gospel Luke tells us 'There were two others with him, criminals who were being led away to execution; and when they reached the place called The Skull, they crucified him there, and the criminals with him, one on his right and the other on his left. Jesus said, "Father, forgive them; they do not know what they are doing."'

They crucified him. They separated him from society.

The problem of the last words appears when Christ is in his solitude, forcibly separated from society. There are other moments in the Gospels where Christ quite deliberately separates himself from society and his companions. His intention at these moments is clear. It is usually to clarify his mind with regard to some moral problem such as the testing-time he spent alone in the wilderness before his comments on the nature of power. There was the time of agony when he separated himself from the others in the garden of Gethsemane just before they judged him, when he prayed 'Father, if it be thy will, take this cup away from me. Yet not my will but thine be done.' (Luke 22: 42)

But here there is no moral problem—for him. He is alone, even though a thief hangs to his right and another to his left. All through the Gospels his teaching has been concrete, in a situation; there is continually a setting in life. The parables, the morals, the miracles all spring from real situations, from character, people aware of themselves in sickness and health, in poverty and wealth.

The difference here is that while the situation on the cross is still within life, being the result of a legal process, the resolution of that process, the penalty that followed the judgment, the price of the pattern of the life he had proved by living it, this situation was ultimately to be in solitude.

Christ in solitude, God in solitude, man in solitude. The last words must be seen as a pattern of faith for each person face to his own face in solitude.

The second part of the problem appears when we ask who tells us that Christ on the cross said 'Father, forgive them; they do not know what they are doing.' It is Luke, author of the third Gospel. Luke, like Paul and the other evangelists, was not present at the Crucifixion; he composed his Gospel anything from thirty to fifty years after the event. How he knew this word we do not know; it appears only in his Gospel, which is the third. He may have heard it from someone who was there (from Mary, the mother of Jesus?), he may have read it (in *Quelle*, the supposed lost source of the New Testament story?). It is said he wrote his Gospel in Greece, in which case the words make some sense, since to the Greeks Christianity was 'folly'.

The point is that no matter how much we may speculate on these matters we are not going to arrive at the sort of significant truth that is persuasive, not the sort of truth that involves us in a fresh understanding of ourselves, that gives concreteness to something we have always known.

Indeed, the apparent carelessness in the reporting of the last words (not one Gospel contains them all) has an increased persuasion because we are familiar with this casual process in our experience. We wish that things would happen logically like the alphabet; we can control our movement from, say, point A to point B. We cannot control or predict the contingency which invalidates our systematic philosophy, weakens all generalizations and presents our understanding with the need for choice.

All that a Christian is asked to believe is that 'the eternal truth, God, has come into being in time, has been born like everyone else, has grown up like everyone else, and so on and so forth' (Kierkegaard). Given the universal and eternal sense in which we use the word God, this Christian belief is incomprehensible; it was 'folly' to the Greeks, and a 'stumbling block' to the Jews. And yet if we are to understand the completely novel nature of the Christian insight we must see that, except to Christ himself, God's appearance in time was absolutely contingent to all history and to all mankind. It is of the essence of the insight that it was unpredictable. The cross is a symbol of the suffering by which God reveals Himself; the last words are the means by which the contingent continually reasserts itself. The situation and the words together, because we know them, are predictably unpredictable, in that they force us to that which we would avoid—to choose. Not once only, but every time we confront the cross, a choice must be made.

If we then are to make significant sense of the last words God uttered in solitude on the cross, we in our solitude must choose decisively to bring them into our self knowledge. And if we humbly ask why Christ said this word, and why Luke reported it, we might see why we must choose it as the first word uttered from the cross.

'Father, forgive them; they do not know what they are doing.'

We know what Christ said; do we understand how to appropriate what he said? Seven words spread over four Gospels, one word alone reported in two Gospels (Mark and Matthew), the other six words reported in equal number by the other evangelists, three in Luke, three in John. There is no logical process here, no philosophical premise leading through a succession of arguments to a conclusion which sustains and explains the premise, no linear progression, as the craftsmen hands the secrets of his craft to his son. How might we view what Luke and the other evangelists are doing? If we are to make our personal choice of these words in appropriating them inwardly to ourselves they must appear to us as a pattern, a coherent pattern to which we give a logical significance by our own choice. We must choose them as a mosaic as it were, at the centre of which is Christ on the cross. This, Luke understood, and in his characteristic mode of reconciliation by reason of the emotions he chose this word as his first word.

Christ is in this situation by himself. Luke understood this and recognized that with the self, even Christ's self, even God's self, the ground must be cleared if a movement is first to be made inwards in understanding. It has been said that Christianity is spirit, spirit is inwardness.

'Father, forgive them; they do not know what they are doing.'

The special characteristic of the religion called

Christianity is that its revelation of God is primarily through dialogue—dialogue between God and man. This is true of its background in the Old Testament, and it is present in the Gospels. It is present also in Paul in the letters, but in a different sense. We must remember that Paul is dealing with the consequences of the revelation of Christianity, not the revelation itself. There is no indication in any of the letters that Paul was aware of the last words. To Paul the cross was the symbol of coherence of all material and spiritual life. 'But God forbid that I should boast of anything but the cross of our Lord Jesus Christ, through which the world is crucified to me and I to the world.' he wrote in his letter to the Galatians (6 : 14).

A meditation on Good Friday for us is concerned with the particular and concrete revelation of God through the last words of a man hanging on a cross. Why did Christ say these words?

'Father, forgive them; they do not know what they are doing.'

Of all people who might understand what isolation on a cross meant, it would certainly be Christ, that is if God was to reveal Himself in his and our freedom. There could not be a situation further removed from all the claims that had been made by Greek or Jew about God, His power and so on. We can live this situation in our imagination; Christ lived concretely the thing itself. The difference is absolute. The gulf between our imagination and reality measures our humility in the presence of Christ's situation.

Ours is the task of accepting his situation of solitude, of being a pattern of experience that we must all follow, of a mosaic of which he was at the centre, of what must first be done if that isolation, that pattern, that mosaic was to have a continuing life, and not harden into a crystalline inflexibility. Whatever he was to do and reveal about himself he first had to do something about the external world. This Luke saw. This we must see.

If the first word does not proclaim his own particular triumph over the world insofar as that world might congratulate itself on having defeated him and thus destroyed his constant charity to others, then the danger is that anything that follows might be seen as surrender, as self-pity, as despair, as an ingratiating meekness, as the gentle havering of a deluded carpenter.

There must be a sense of inner control. There might be poignant tears and suffering, but there must be no invitation to sentiment. The words must be objectively appropriate to his self-awareness of the situation.

And the triumph must be such that it could be recognized in his terms, in the terms to himself that was the triumph, not in terms imposed by the world. He had already accepted these; he was hanging on a cross. He could have judged the world, and those who judged him. He could have cursed them as they cursed him. He could have deserted the world and forgotten it as he was deserted and forgotten. It was not necessary for the world for Christ to forgive it. It was absolutely necessary for himself for without this word he could not begin the inner revelation of the cross, the particular revelation which Paul knew nothing about, that we know, that is the essential nature of Christianity. (I mean the particularity of the last words from the cross.)

By this word Christ declares that he is in command of himself. Anything else that he might have said at this moment would have been an acceptance, a surrender, a curse, a judgment, a finality. Of the seven words we must come on this one first. It clears the ground for something more.

Instead of turning away from the cross as we might have done had we to our shame been judged, as we in our self-satisfaction and power have been cursed, as we in our ignorance have been confused, we are forgiven, and we look at one being crucified in astonishment and wonder, at one who, completely powerless, forgave.

There has been considerable controversy as to the nature of grace. Is it not possible that we might see this first word of Christ's from the cross as the first movement of grace in action expressed by Christ in action since without it there can be no movement or dialogue between men? Might we so regard it as we peer at him and hear the words; 'Father, . . .'

How does he begin his dialogue? He begins by placing his action in the sphere to which it belongs—the ethical. Christ in the New Testament continually appeals to the Father. The evangelists in composing the life understood this, as it was part of their Jewish heritage. Judaism is profoundly an ethical religion in that the relations between Jehovah and the race are always superior to the relations between Jehovah and the individual. Indeed it is only recently that the question could be asked in Israel 'Who is a Jew?' Unlike Greek thought, there is no ontological problem in Judaism, just as to the Jew there is no philosophical difference between appearance and reality. It is the Greeks, following Socrates, who have provided European philosophers with the main grounds for their inquiries into ontology, the nature of being, and the nature of objective knowledge as it hovers between appearance and reality.

The Jew leads a moral life because he subscribes to the primacy of the covenant between Jehovah and the race, a covenant which solved for the Jews the problem of ethics. To the Greeks the facts of the moral life were always a matter for debate, because there was never general agreement on the nature of the state.

Christ's offence to Judaism and the Greeks lay in his revelation of God as a relationship between person and person, going beyond the race, and the state.

The power of Christ's insights as revealed by the evangelists consisted in his constant awareness of what belonged to the individual and what pertained to the race. Forgiveness is a process within law. The appeal therefore must be within law, within the ethics of the race, to the Father. Not to God.

'Father, forgive them . . .'

There were so many and there were too many diverse acts to be forgiven, from the immediate disciples who abandoned him to those who unfairly judged him, to those like Pilate who recognized his innocence yet in response to the demand of the mob still judged him. We could build up a list of monstrous sins and omissions, but we must keep our eyes on Christ.

Forgiveness in this situation is an act of will, a will which in the matter of forgiveness is natural to him but which we can exercise only by effort.

We say forgive and forget, he said forgive and then he forgot—because he does not mention those things again. They belong to his past, and they must not be allowed to impinge on his present. We can never be sure that our frail memories will not remind us of what we should have forgotten because our wills are never constantly in our control. With him it is otherwise; his will is constantly within his control.

'Father, forgive them; they do not know what they are doing.'

With hindsight we may wonder at the pity of it. Did they know what they were doing to God Himself? We may go further and suggest that if one so behaved today he might suffer the same fate. This is pointless. What we are to understand here is the need for self-awareness in what we are doing carelessly, from one who knew precisely what he was doing. And if we continue the ethical strain in which this word is held, he is pointing to the need for self-awareness as a release from the dominance of thoughtless repetition, from the safe institutions we evolve to maintain society, from the sober structures we fabricate in which to lead our lives.

In this first word we are to understand what is urgently needed as the first movement towards self-knowledge now.

O Lord Jesus Christ, would that we also might be contemporary with Thee, see Thee in Thy true form in the actual environment in which Thou didst walk here on earth: not in the form in which an empty and meaningless tradition, or a thoughtless and superstitious, or a gossipy historical tradition, has deformed Thee: for it is not in the form of abasement the believer sees Thee, and it cannot possibly be in the form of glory, in which no man has yet seen Thee. Would that we might see Thee as Thou art and wast and wilt be until Thy return in glory, see Thee as the sign of offence and the object of faith, the lowly man, and yet the Saviour and Redeemer of the race, who out of love came to earth in order to seek the lost, in order to suffer and to die, and yet sorely troubled as Thou wast, alas, at every step Thou didst take upon earth, every time Thou didst stretch out Thy hand to perform signs and wonders, and every time, without moving a hand, Thou didst suffer defencelessly the opposition of men—again and again Thou wast constrained to repeat: Blessed is he whosoever is not offended in Me. Would that we might see Thee thus, and then that for all this we might not be offended in Thee.

SØREN KIERKEGAARD

THE SECOND WORD

I tell you this: today you shall be with me in Paradise.

Luke 23: 43

ONE of the criminals who hung there with him taunted him: '"Are not you the Messiah? Save yourself, and us." But the other rebuked him: "Have you no fear of God? You are under the same sentence as he. For us it is plain justice; we are paying the price for our misdeeds; but this man has done nothing wrong." And he said, "Jesus, remember me when you come to your throne." He answered; "I tell you this: today you shall be with me in Paradise."'

Again it is only Luke who gives us this word from the cross, and we may note that whereas the first word was expressed as a generalization to the world, the dialogue here is more particular, directed to those in the immediate vicinity. In the mosaic we are composing of the last words the movement is inwards to the final moment of solitude and suffering. Here, we are invited to look for some deeper purpose beyond the simplicity of the dialogue, as if the evangelist were introducing himself into the situation to direct our attention as to how we might view it.

The first thief asks; 'Are not you the Messiah? Save yourself, and us.'

The second thief answers him, 'Have you no fear of God? You are under the same sentence as he. For us it is plain justice; we are paying the price of our misdeeds, but this man has done nothing wrong.' He now turns to Jesus and says 'Jesus, remember me when you come to your throne', to which Christ replies, 'I tell you this: today you shall be with me in Paradise.'

Now clearly, Luke is not such a fool, nor can he deem us so uncritical, as to expect us to accept this dialogue at its face value. He is writing his Gospel some thirty to fifty years after the event, and is alone of the evangelists to go into this detail. And yet he reports the words as though he had heard them at first hand; they are so vivid and psychologically apt. Two thousand years after the event, when it has become saturated with overtones, it is easy for us to read into it our thoughts and desires that even in this extremity the divinity of Christ was recognized by a thief.

No, no; if we are to understand this situation as one revealing the hidden God the obvious interpretation is not what Luke means; hiddenness does not reveal itself directly; there is no place in the New Testament where Christ ever proclaims his identity as Moses heard Jehovah proclaim 'I am that I am'; the most Christ would say about himself was 'Blessed is he whosoever is not offended in me.' Nor can it be that Luke is inviting us to admire Christ at this point; that would be childish. Admiration is an incidental attribute to Christ; it is not the essential ground by which one is held, a consequence of which is that coherence which an individual, fully aware of himself, finds with the world. 'Remember me when you come to your throne.'

The thief goes on too long, and is too reasonable. A thief talking to a man hanging by him on another cross, a thief objectively perceiving so much, he cannot be ironic—for we must remember that the coming of the Holy Spirit, when men's eyes were opened as to what the New Testament was about and how it was accomplished, did not occur until Pentecost, fifty days later, 'Men of Israel, listen to me: I speak of Jesus of Nazareth, a man singled out by God and made known to you through miracles, portents, and signs, which God worked among you through him as you well know.' As Peter knew, but the thief hanging next to Christ on the cross, did he know? And Luke, coming after, knew. It is to Luke we must turn if we are to understand this word and perhaps advance a little in the understanding of the revelation of the hidden God.

'I tell you this, today, you shall be with me in Paradise.'

We have noted that the revelation of the New Testament is in a setting in life; in concrete situations through characters in despair and sickness. Nor is it merely that we are listening to moral precepts given by a man so that we may live a good life. The life in its setting is composed in retrospect, it emerges as a dialogue between Christ and the evangelists. We have to understand not only what Christ's life is about but how the evangelists are composing it. For even in this extreme situation of the cross Christ cannot reveal himself directly to the world; and this is the special characteristic of Christianity, its indirectness. We cannot understand the consequences of Christianity without Paul and his special temperament, so we cannot understand the pattern of the Gospels without understanding the imaginative insights which the evangelists variously bring. Why should the seven last words be spread quite arbitrarily over the four Gospels? Why should Luke alone be concerned with what I think we should see as the first two words unless they correspond to his intuitive grasp of the sort of contribution he was making to the picture of the whole life?

Take the birth of Christ, for instance. Mark does not notice it, but jumps immediately into the prophetic background out of which the New Testament emerges. Matthew takes Joseph's part and recounts the child's ancestry. Luke leans to Mary; there is a tradition that he had it from the Virgin herself. John, like Paul, seizes on the theology of the life, 'In the beginning was the Word, and the Word was with God, and the Word was God.'

Mark, Matthew, Luke, Acts, John. The New Testament grows in density from the essential simplicity of Mark to the sophisticated embroideries of John. Between is Luke reconciling, continually reconciling, reconciling the life to the literature, reconciling the revelation to the consequences in Acts, and reconciling us to the offence, the offence of the God-man. It is Luke who brings the emotional threads of the life together in the image of the 'pierced heart'.

The thing to be noted in reading the Gospels is that what seems basically simple is always basically complex, precisely because there is always a minimum of two views. We long for an intellectual harmony, a simple unity which will embrace our understanding of the world, but Christianly speaking this can never be. There is always a minimum of two views.

Nowhere is this more crucial than the Christian's understanding of the nature of offence. Without some understanding of offence we shall not grasp how Christianity reveals God's intervention in the world.

The first word is placed firmly in the ethical world, in Judaism. The second word is the first movement beyond the ethical toward the religious; it bodies forth the saying that God did not deem it above Himself to be reckoned among criminals. Why?

Christ said to the thief, 'Today you shall be with me in Paradise.' The central message of the New Testament which must be grasped in all its shocking severity is that God made Christ the cursed one for us. Each of us must add in his inwardness—*for me.*

'Cursed is the man that hangs on a tree'—the saying is as old as Deuteronomy. Paul repeats it in his letter to the Galatians (3 : 13) 'Christ redeemed us from the curse of the law' by becoming the cursed one himself. It is the perverse psychological insight that caught the imagination of the first Christians. From this Paul can go on to hold the symbol of the cross as central to his understanding of the suffering universe 'through which the world is crucified to me, and I to the world.' Without this offence Christianity cannot move beyond the law to the heart of its revelation, which is concerned in the first instance with the individual and how a person is related in solitude to the universe. This paradox precedes dogmatic and doctrinal commitments.

'Today you shall be with me in Paradise.'

Heaven is a Christian generalisation for the unknown, given philosophical standing by Greek thought, and it is through Plato's doctrine of the immortality of the soul that later Christianity can identify heaven with Paradise. The New Testament uses the word immortality only three times, the Jews never at all. The notion of immortality sits very uneasily next to offence, and we must not interpret the word Paradise as a finality so that it removes the innate contradiction of the situation or the decisiveness of the statement, 'Today you shall be with me——' No, Paradise is the unknown, the unknown out of which we have our being and recognize ourselves as different. For now we know.

'Today you shall be with me——'

Perhaps there is this to be said for the penitent thief, as it might be said for everyone in suddenly apprehending what an eternal solitude might mean; that he suddenly recognized the freedom to do something different from what he had ever done before. For one moment he was totally revealed in his impotence on the cross and he longingly wished (unlike Christ) for company. 'Jesus, remember me when you come to your throne.' Now, only now, might we see the irony, the use of that word 'throne'. But it goes unnoticed. The thief was free to recognize that far from being an illusion it was in the highest sense a deadly reality, in that he was assured by God Himself, so he thought, that he would be with him in death. As it is for us all.

'Today you shall be with me—with me—with me—'

Oh! Wonderful, wonderful! That the one who has help to give is the one who says, Come hither! What love is this! There is love in the act of a man who is able to help and does help him who begs for help. But for one to offer help! and to offer it to all! Yes, and precisely to all such as can do nothing to help in return! To offer it—no, to shout it out, as if the Helper were the one who needed help, as if in fact He who is able and willing to help all was Himself in a sense a needy one, in that he feels an urge, and consequently need to help, need of the sufferer in order to help him!

SØREN KIERKEGAARD

THE THIRD WORD

Woman, behold thy son!
Behold thy mother.

John 19:27

IN the mosaic of understanding the Pattern of the Life of the New Testament we now choose to turn to John. It is only in his Gospel, the fourth Gospel, that we have this word.

'But meanwhile near the cross where Jesus hung stood his mother, with her sister, Mary wife of Clopas, and Mary of Magdala. Jesus saw his mother, with the disciple whom he loved standing by her. He said to her, "Mother, there is your son"; and to the disciple, "There is your mother"; and from that moment the disciple took her into his home.'

So the translation in the New English Bible, and its justification lies in that the words so translated satisfy the Church's theological concept of the Atonement, a desire sustained by the evangelist's own theological tendency. I prefer the Authorized Version of 1611. It is more severe, unambiguous and immediate.

'Woman, behold thy son!' 'Behold thy mother.' Mary, his mother, is at the cross.

We began our meditation on the situation of the cross by suggesting that Christ himself recognized that his teaching, even at this extreme moment, must begin in the reality of the external world. It moves inwards as his attention is drawn to the two thieves who are hanging by his side. Now his look is forward, he sees his mother. With absolute truthfulness he can say, 'Woman, behold thy son!'

And then?—— And then what?

Given this situation of extreme agony is it psychologically appropriate that he should now direct his mind away from his mother and instruct a disciple, even the one whom he is supposed to have loved best, to behold her, and take her into his care? Is it not possible, just possible that the various traditions oral and otherwise which transmit the substance of the pattern of the New Testament might at this moment pause in humility—for humility is at the heart of this word—as Christ still with his eyes on his mother, murmurs to himself, 'Behold thy mother.'

Nothing, it seems to me, at this moment should be allowed to diminish the harsh reality of their relationship now.

It is possible that John, writing his Gospel some say about the year 100, or at any rate a considerable time after the event, wished to give the word a significance beyond the bleak statement of fact, and interpolates the piece about the 'disciple standing by' who out of compassion took her into his house. It is not merely out of character for the disciples, who are always thought of with the houseless poor, but worse, it blunts our imaginative response to the situation of Mary.

John is the most theologically inclined of the evangelists, and theology, the science of God, in its desire for a unity and coherence of doctrine, seeks after notions of redemption and salvation which stun the penitent, whose only intention at the cross is to listen.

'Woman, behold thy son!' 'Behold thy mother.'

This is the word from the cross that assures us, that Christ's mother was there. The disciples were absent; they had all fled, but his mother was there. There is an almost wilful ambiguity in the number of Marys who were there!—Mary of Magdala, Mary the wife of Clopas. . . . It is John's artistry to introduce them here so that he can recall them at a moment more appropriate to his purpose, that is in the resurrection literature of which John's is the most abundant witness. And yet in all that literature, and not only in John's, while Christ appears to many he never discloses himself to his mother. She of all who were concerned there, it might be thought, would be given some reassurance. But no, in all his appearances, and among those attending the sepulchre there is no mention of his mother. There are plenty of Marys, but no reference precisely pointed to his mother. We must now look closely elsewhere; we must look at Mary.

'Mother, behold thy son!' 'Behold thy mother.'

The evangelists are so sure in composing their life of Christ that it would be impertinent to suggest that John has missed out something that we are discovering, about the mother of God. The nature of the hidden God can never be revealed directly. The discovery of offence by the evangelists—that God made Christ the cursed one for us—transforms the New Testament from a descriptive exercise in words to a searching experience of the ambiguity of life. We must note the revealing omissions.

There are times when the evangelists repeat each other with slight variations, and there are times when each evangelist includes a particular incident that corresponds to his temperament. John must have recalled what Luke (who wrote before him) tells us about the birth and the subsequent events, Luke, whose special concern is Mary. It is Luke who tells us what Mary said when she was told that she would conceive:

'Tell out, my soul, the greatness of the Lord,
rejoice, rejoice, my spirit, in God my saviour;
so tenderly has he looked upon his servant,
humble as she is . . .'

It is Luke who tells us what happened when they brought Jesus to Jerusalem to present him to the Lord.

'There was at that time in Jerusalem a man called Simeon. This man was upright and devout, one who watched and waited for the restoration of Israel, and the Holy Spirit was upon him. It had been disclosed to him by the Holy Spirit that he would not see death until he had seen the Lord's Messiah. Guided by the Spirit he came into the temple; and when the parents brought the child Jesus to do for him what was customary under the Law, he took him in his arms, praised God, and said:

'This day, Master, thou givest thy servant his
discharge in peace;
now thy promise is fulfilled.
For I have seen with my own eyes
the deliverance which thou hast made ready in full
view of all the nations;
A light that will be a revelation to the heathen,
and glory to thy people Israel.'

The child's father and mother were full of wonder at what was being said about him. Simeon blessed them and said to Mary his mother, "This child is destined to be a sign which men reject; and you too shall be pierced to the heart. Many in Israel will stand or fall because of him, and thus the secret thoughts of many will be laid bare."'

'You too shall be pierced to the heart.'

While we accept John's suggestion that indeed Christ may have in mind the beloved disciple, is it not possible that in Mary's mind there are the words she once heard from Simeon, 'And this shall be a sign which men reject,' and in the most intimate sense Christ is recalling to her what was predicted, that she will be pierced to the heart.

'Woman, behold thy son.'

This was contrary to everything that had been predicted for her otherwise. The mother of God? The chosen one? Was she humble enough to believe this? Had Mary said anything at this moment to dissolve the tension the distinctive feature of Christianity would not have been conveyed, that it is silent suffering. Christianity cannot be lived without a pierced heart.

'Behold thy mother.'

In a sense the last words can only be understood as God talking to himself. Not as a madman talks to himself and so reveals that he is cut off from everyone around. No, it is God talking, and we listen. We are astounded. Impaled on a cross, unjustly or justly, but impaled on a cross his first thought, so we choose it, is for others, and he forgives them. How can one possibly do this in this situation? But that is to lose oneself in admiration of the action, and in our admiration forget that although the action is something to wonder at, it is the person who performs it who holds our attention.

At least we are beginning to see perhaps as we meditate on these words and give them our own order that it involves an understanding of Christ's isolation as he moved inwards to himself. And as we approach his isolation so there is a movement inwards in ourselves as our hearts, like Mary's, are pierced.

This is a new understanding of a new spirit of a new inwardness. Into me, not in the exclusive sense that it is available to me only, but that it is available to me absolutely alone, to me and no-one else. This is the wonder of it—it is, such is its quality, communicable to all if they are like Mary before the cross, and continually before the cross.

I cannot think of the last words as Alfred North Whitehead describes them—'the gentle words from the cross, as life ebbed away.' The judgment and patronage of God is a fearsome thing when one thinks of it truly. If one can, and not get lost in the easy generalisation that what was happening here has passed into the understanding, creation has moved on from Calvary at a specific moment; the unceasing motion of the universe has expressed itself, and change has brought into being as a constant acceptable reference the God of theology, the monotheistic concept of the Jews as it emerges over centuries cannot be concerned with this moment of time, for in eternity all seconds are equal. But not this one. This second is eternally different.

'Woman, behold thy son.' 'Behold thy mother.'

The word makes a difference. Universally all human

beings are subjects—to God. That's what this word means. We are brought face to face with subjects seeking a particularity. Mary is a subject to Christ, her son; Christ is a subject to Mary, his mother. They are not objects, one to the other, but subjects, persons if you like the word better. With this word we move from the external world of things, of objects like crosses and concepts of Paradise. We are shedding the general world of people . . . of 'them', of judges, deserters, thieves, of the establishment.

There are two ways in which a subject is to be understood. The first is as a man or a woman, a wife or husband, a father or mother, a son or daughter. As he or she is born so they are born into a generality of the race which has been present in the world since recorded time. There is a secondary understanding of a subject, that it is given to each subject to understand his or her particularity, having a sex, a name, but also a setting in life uniquely individual and absolutely separate from all other uniquely individual subjects in the universe.

This word from the cross focuses in the most concrete manner the situation of two people within a given history. We can understand the first two words from the cross simply enough in the sense that Christ's forgiveness was an act of grace before he could start to reveal the nature of the Christian spirit. We can understand Christ's relation to the thieves as a contingent event which he could not predict but which he faced and immediately solved in the most gracious way possible. His assurance of companionship was the most truthful and real blessing he could offer to the thieves at the moment of death.

Here is a different situation.

We know the history of these two people. We have read the Gospels and we have arrived at that part which is called 'the final conflict'. We have been told of the virgin birth, of the promises made to Mary. We have lived through two years of teaching and work, expressing the pattern of the Christian life. It has come to this. A son on a cross facing his mother. Behold—look—see. Everything has been stripped away, the glory, the magnification, even the humility at this moment has been scraped away.

These two are as it were naked before each other. I mean nakedness in the sense that there is no worldly contrivance even if they desired it to shield them from the blazing purity of each other, from the thing of being. We are in the presence of being, pure being, the thing itself. It is now being revealed to us how the movement of God works in a mind that has not as yet the benefit of eternity. We must always start from where we are, rooted in reality, in life, in our situation. We cannot begin with thought. The only person who can begin with thought and lead to being is God. This, it seems to me, Christ had to assure us of as he moved from reality into himself. He understood his mother—his first and last touch with reality—well enough to test her to understand his situation in the fulness of her time. Mary was silent.

'Woman, behold thy son.' 'Behold thy mother.'

Christ is the truth in such a sense that to be the truth is the only true explanation of what the truth is. Hence one may ask an Apostle, one may ask a Christian, what truth is, and then the Apostle or the Christian will point to Christ and say, 'Behold Him, learn of Him, He was the truth.' That is to say, the truth, in the sense in which Christ was the truth, is not a sum of sentences, not a definition of concepts, etc., but a life.

And hence, Christianly understood, the truth consists not in knowing the truth but in being the truth.

SØREN KIERKEGAARD

THE FOURTH WORD

I thirst.

John 19: 28

'AFTER that, Jesus, aware that all now had come to its appointed end, said, in fulfilment of Scripture, "I thirst."'

In the mosaic of the pattern of the life of the New Testament we turn again to John. In his character as the theologian of the evangelists he not only gives the word a history and place, but he introduces us to a new element—the physical awareness of Jesus. Jesus, aware that all now had come to its appointed end.

The mark of the life in spite of the contradictions which the evangelists introduce in the telling of it is its enormous coherence from beginning to end. We are continually dominated in our lives by the contingency of events, we are open and vulnerable to the uncertainty which flaws our best intentions and scatters our wishes to the winds. We cannot predict with certainty, we cannot foresee that which we must avoid.

There does not seem any time in his life when Jesus was not in command of his environment. Nor do the evangelists ever seek to contrive a situation falsely to his advantage. His self-knowledge is complete, his will comes naturally to him; our self-knowledge comes by will.

'I thirst.'

In continuance of giving the words from the cross a movement from the external world inwards we choose to place this word here in the mosaic, as it is the only word referring to the sheer physical reaction to the agony, the pain of the man on the cross. Physical pain precedes spiritual pain because it is lesser, it is of lower value than spiritual pain. Gloucester's eyes are gouged out before Lear loses his mind.

When the body is under great strain the reaction is felt at its most acute in the mouth. The most sensitive part of the mouth, the tongue, goes dry. When the mind is fearful, so that the imagination seizes on its unexpected freedom to indulge in terrifying dreams and horrible possibilities, again the body responds to this in the mouth. When the nerves are stretched beyond endurance the throat is parched, the tongue dries up and thirst follows.

This thirst is private to the person in pain, it cannot be communicated feelingly to anyone. However imaginative our sympathy with Christ in his agony this thirst cannot be reproduced in our bodies. Those who reproduce the stigmata lack what is needful here . . . the cross, and the suffering understanding of physical pain which precedes spiritual pain.

'I thirst.'

Our real task before the cross is to recognize our solitude there. From now on he is solitary. The first three words have served their purpose. We have seen Christ in his setting in life, we have seen that setting dissolve to its residue of suffering. That is what remains, what we are free to observe. Suffering. But what kind of suffering?

This is the first word from the cross that opens the way to a direct relationship with Christ, and it is in a mode I can begin to understand by suffering. Up to now pain has certainly been there, but so have others. The whole of mankind was there, and two thieves were there, and his mother was there. Now I have moved forward and there is no-one else, no-one but me. We are alone with Christ, you and I.

Can it be that if I am to understand the spiritual nature of what is being revealed it must somehow begin with suffering? Whose suffering—Christ's or mine? Clearly it cannot be mine, since I am not in a position privileged to suffer, being merely an observer at the cross. Again, if by the projection of my imagination I place myself alongside Christ and as it were live his suffering vicariously can I really be sure that what I feel is not due to some internal need of my own, a self-indulgence, and so I deceive myself?

Up to now we have been able to shield ourselves from the impact of the man on the cross by turning towards those who were with him. Now we are alone, it seems we must practise what we have learned from the first three words: that Christianity is a revelation about the hidden God, and that whenever a Christian would know what Christianity is about he must learn that it is about a life. And if he desires he can say this quite simply that 'the eternal truth, God, has come into being in time, has been born like everyone else, has grown up precisely like everyone else, and so on and so forth.' That is a matter of faith, and I have not come to that yet. I am still anxious after self-knowledge.

God and self knowledge. It seems to me that if we are to understand this word we must introduce something new that embraces the man on the cross and the observer, something that unites God and my self-knowledge. Much as a rich man, seeing a poor man unable to do anything because he knew nothing of money, offers him his wealth and makes it possible for the poor man to achieve something.

Suppose the new element that we introduce is something that we have not considered before, and yet it is something that men talk about in Christianity so much that one might think it as cheap as the money was to the rich man. And yet that this new element was not only cheap but removed as far as possible from a man suffering or a Christ saying 'I thirst.' Suppose we introduce the word 'love'. Not in the sense that God is love, that I do not understand yet, but love in the sense of self-knowledge, in the sense that self-love precedes love of the other, in the sense that without love we shall not have that freedom to understand that we are all, but absolutely all, equal before God. And so it has been through all history, in spite of the divinity that men have taken upon themselves, like Caesar Augustus. In spite of the monarchies, the constellations of power that men manufacture to sustain the comfortable structure of their societies, this can be said from the beginning of time, that all men are equal before God. This is where love begins, in recognizing the absolute equality of all men before God. It is only in the most general sense that we can say that God is love, because this love, like equality, has been present from the eternal past and will be present to the eternal future. There is something that equality, love, God, all share, and it is this: they share eternity.

To say in this abstract way that God is love is not to repeat the two direct commands of Christ that dissolve the law—To love God, and our neighbour as ourselves. Both these commands have a specific aim within the Christian revelation, towards God and your neighbour who, at the simplest, is the person next to you. Not the person you choose to be next to you, but one who has been placed there casually as the result of a movement that has been in the world since the beginning of time.

Suppose now we go on to say that the eternity of love is made manifest only through a moment of suffering, such a moment as when a man on a cross says, 'I thirst.' Can we go on from this to say that love is a meaningless abstraction unless it is corrected and disciplined by an inward understanding of the nature of suffering?

'I thirst.'

Until this century war was an immediate thing and a distress signal was quickly answered with a response to relieve the suffering. It is perhaps one of the more regrettable calamities of our age that the mind of man has evolved weapons that can conduct war over great distances. Now that the aggressor is hidden from the victim the distress of war is likely to arouse less response.

One of the few incidents at the cross that is reported in all four gospels is the story that Christ's distress prompted some of the bystanders to offer him sour wine, or vinegar. The evangelists vary as to when it happened, but all declare that something like this took place as the simple, honest response of men who, seeing distress, were anxious to relieve it. What these men did by nature we must do by our choice of will. Everything is calculated in our society to place us at a distance from suffering.

Not that we must desire suffering in the hope that by so doing we might flee the terror 'that suffering is the characteristic of God's love'. We must not lose ourselves in it as a self-indulgence, we must not congratulate ourselves that had we been there we would have benevolently done likewise. What then is to be done at this moment to understand the pattern of the cross? One thing: we can dare—to dare is Christian. It requires little daring to face up to the truths of the external world; they can be proved to the satisfaction of reason, but to dare in the face of this situation to recognize that truth lies in a life 'even when we see that the suffering is, humanly speaking, unavoidable; just go on and dare.' (Kierkegaard)

In the task of becoming a Christian, love and suffering must be held together. They cannot be separated, except at this moment, when the evangelists in composing the life give us the particular steps when we can give a body to the symbol—the symbol which Paul alone knew.

Take Paul. To him the cross was the symbol of a crucifixion which gave coherence and unity to a movement outwards from himself to the world, and from the world inwards to himself. Outwards to the world in love, and inwards to himself in suffering.

One of the great insights which Paul is anxious to impress on those to whom he writes his letters is the duality in human awareness. There is the impatient body with its needs and desires, and there is the transcendent spirit which informs the quality of the satisfactions. Between recognizing the need and the quality of satisfaction man's growth to maturity will be measured. To Paul, only by Christ, through Christ and in Christ can the physical and the spiritual be reconciled, and the measure of the reconciliation is the individual's awareness, as Paul put it, of 'Not I, but Christ liveth in me.' This is something the Greeks did not know. Until Socrates they felt they were at the mercy of external pressures, and even when Socrates personified the unknown in God as the source of self-awareness the insight lay in the field of knowledge rather than as with Paul in the field of religious freedom and choice.

Paul could assert with absolute certainty that 'not I but Christ liveth in me', not merely because it was a choice made in freedom—he had not known Christ in life and was not particularly anxious to glean any information about him from the disciples—but because it reflected an act of will that lay outside the ethical, outside the law of Judaism; an act of will that lay in the solitary field of the religious, where everyman finds himself having to make sense of the universe and his own setting in life.

'I thirst.'

As Paul reached for the symbol of the cross we reach for the word. Two thousand years separate us from Christ. We cannot like the onlookers assuage his thirst with a sponge dipped in vinegar, but we can be astonished at this word which falls so unpredictably from the lips of one who, if I am to be a Christian, is 'the eternal truth, God' who 'has come into being in time, has been born like everyone else, has grown up precisely like everyone else, and so on, and so forth.' And we can dare to go on, as a mother suffering a pierced heart dared to go on and listen. As Mary was there, so am I, so is each one of us.

'I thirst.'

And I begin to see in a new way that we are all equal. Had Paul and the disciples known the last words of the cross as we now know them then they would have had an advantage in that they heard the words from God Himself, revealing Himself directly. But this is precisely what cannot be done in Christianity, which is concerned with the revelation of the hidden God. The most a contemporary of Christ could do was to touch him to make sure that he lived, when he died the most succeeding generations could do was to listen. Where faith is concerned the disciples who were his contemporaries have no advantage over the succeeding generations who came after and listened. Indeed, the evangelists realised this in that without the resurrection how could the disciples know that Christianity is a communication about a life. The abashed disciples who had fled from Jesus did not, like Mary, hear the last words; hence the need as the evangelists saw for the resurrection literature.

There is no priority here. There is a choice. We may come to the life by the symbol of the cross, we may listen to the words. We are free to choose either. To those who are listening to the words from now on the adventure of discovering the self by the self is open to us.

There is an endless yawning difference between God and man, and hence, in the situation of contemporaneousness, to become a Christian (to be transformed into likeness with God) proved to be an even greater torment and misery and pain than the greatest human torment, and hence also a crime in the eyes of one's neighbours. And so it will always prove when becoming a Christian in truth comes to mean to become contemporary with Christ. And if becoming a Christian does not come to mean this, then all the talk about becoming a Christian is nonsense and self-deception and conceit, in part even blasphemy and sin against the Second Commandment of the Law and sin against the Holy Ghost.

SØREN KIERKEGAARD

THE FIFTH WORD

My God, my God, why hast thou forsaken me?

Mark 15: 34
Matthew 27: 46

'At midday a darkness fell over the whole land, till three in the afternoon; and at three Jesus cried aloud "Eli, Eli, lema sabachthani," which, means, "My God, my God, why hast thou forsaken me?"'

It is the first word we hear from the cross as recounted only, and it alone, by Mark and Matthew, but in the mosaic of the pattern of the life we choose it as central.

William Barclay in his translation has Jesus shouting at the top of his voice, 'My God, My God, why have you abandoned me?'

The words are a mixture of Hebrew and Aramaic. They figure first in the Greek Bible. Greek was the original language of the New Testament. In the fourth century, when Jerome translated the Bible into Latin, the words were retained in the original, so also when the Vulgate was translated into the vernacular. Because of this there is a strong feeling that we are listening to the words Christ actually used. Whether this is so or not there is certainly a sense in which this one word is not merely the central word from the cross, but also the Archimedean point on which Christianity is balanced. If there is any doubt about the humanity of

God in Christ this word dispels it. We are face to face with the most extreme situation of a human being.

'My God, my God, why hast thou forsaken me?'

The onlookers were uncertain of what they heard. Mark tells us that 'some of the bystanders on hearing this, said, "Hark, he is calling Elijah." A man came running with a sponge soaked in sour wine, on the end of a cane, and held it to his lips. "Let us see", he said "if Elijah will come to take him down." '

The confusion is understandable. The Greek word for Elijah is Elias, and so the passer-by might for a moment have been confused into a misunderstanding. Coming after all that had been said about Christ (but not by himself) and his teaching, to hear this word in truth must certainly have been inexplicable. Even today it is a point of embarrassment for many Christians who only want to pass as quickly as possible through Good Friday. Yet if there is one moment of truth for Christ in all his life it is here and now—for us it will be continually here and continually now.

There are some who would explain this word away by suggesting that Christ is merely repeating a phrase from the Old Testament, from the 22nd Psalm, which begins 'My God, my God, why hast thou forsaken me?'

Apart from the concrete difference in the situation of the psalmist, who is describing it, and Christ, who is living it, the great danger in holding fast to this explanation is that we are applying absolutely human categories to Christ, for if we talk absolutely humanly about Christ at this moment we would have to admit that the words of extreme despair are untrue. They can only (such is the nature of any concept of God) be true if God says them, and consequently the God-man.

Father . . . Mother . . . God.

It is easy at this moment, overwhelmed by the emotion of the words, to bow our heads and surrender our feelings to wonder and pity. But if there is anything in our view that the last words were uttered by a man completely aware of what he was saying and in full charge of his will we must peer at this precise word more closely than any other because it sums up in its brevity the total difference between God and man, and must be said before any movement can be made to reconcile the difference.

Father . . . Mother . . . God.

In two of his previous words Christ has addressed himself to his Father and his mother. Both these words were, like the law, contained within the ethical sphere that is within a human situation; they expressed a relationship between two people. Now we have moved into the religious sphere, if religion is concerned with how a man relates himself to the universe and to his self-beginning with the unknown. It is in this sense that primitive tribes, the Greeks and the Jews have all used the word God. It is how Christ uses it in the New Testament.

God . . . the unknown.

The first objective view of the nature of personal truth and the unknown using the word God is given by Socrates. When the theogony of the Greek world collapsed at the end of the fifth century as the result of the attacks by the Greek dramatists and the defeat of

Athens in the Peloponnesian War there was no ground for personal identity. Socrates in his solitude perceived that virtue lay in insight into himself; at the same time parallel with this insight he saw truth as something to be learned as an object of inquiry. There lay a difficulty in that 'for what a man knows he cannot seek since he knows it, and what he does not know he cannot seek, since he does not even know for what to seek. Socrates thinks the difficulty through and presents us with the doctrine of Recollection, by which all learning and inquiry is interpreted as a kind of remembering; one who is ignorant needs only a reminder to help him come to himself in the consciousness of what he knows. Thus the truth is not introduced into the individual from without, but was within him. This thought ultimately becomes the point of concentration for the Greek consciousness, since it serves as a proof for the immortality of the soul; but with a backward reference, it is important to note, and hence as a proof of the soul's pre-existence!' (Kierkegaard). It was an enormous leap on the part of Socrates to recognize that the memory only works backwards and the consequences of that for thought.

'Knowledge was recollection, and it was the task of Socrates to bring men to this understanding in themselves, and this activity represented the highest relationship between man and man; even if a divine point of departure is ever given between man and man, this is the true relationship. It was in accordance with Socrates' understanding of the divine principle that his work, though continually under examination by God, lay in bringing men to self-knowledge by themselves.' (Kierkegaard). Knowledge of the truth was recollection from the unknown god which could be described as 'that beauty which always is, never coming into being or passing away, neither growing nor diminishing. It will not be present to the imagination as a face, or hands, or anything which is bodily; nor again as thought or knowledge of any kind, nor does it exist in something other than itself, as in an animal, or in earth or heaven, or anything else, but it always is itself in itself and by itself, sole and unique.'

Plato's description of God has served as a model for a whole range of religious thought from a simple nature worship to the most exquisitely refined tracery of mystical thought. It has provided the ground for philosophers to explain the original impulse of the universe; God as the freely effecting First Cause of Aristotle. And through Aristotle, Aquinas can build his edifice of Christian theology from the Creation through the Fall to the Incarnation and the Atonement, leading to the last things.

It is a use of language unknown to the evangelists as they compose the life of Jesus, and completely inadequate to convey what is being communicated on the cross. It draws our attention to the contrast that must continually be in the Christian's mind; God expressing himself eternally as infinite past and infinite future, and God in time 'who has been born like everyone else, has grown up precisely like everyone else, and so on and so forth.' God in eternity and God in time.

It is at this precise moment, as we hear this word from the cross, that Christ's use of the word God (in distinction to Father) invites us to consider what distinctive proclamation about God the evangelists were concerned to make. For while we recognize that the evangelists were Jews writing within and from a base in Judaism, the dominant mode of thought in Palestine and the Roman Empire was undoubtedly Greek. The Romans about the time of Christ's birth had indirectly confessed their failure to go beyond Greek thought to solve their social and political problems, by taking the retrograde step of deifying the emperor.

Judaism—and the discovery of the Dead Sea scrolls does nothing to contradict this—was held fast in the ethical demands of the Covenant of God with the state. The repetition of ritual and practice stifled movement. The most vital insights into the nature of being at the time of the crucifixion were Greek in origin. Socrates' insight of seeing God as infinitely past, everywhere and nowhere, raised the problem of 'being' for the Greeks and provided a solution in the work of Plato and Aristotle. It is the basis of Greek scepticism that immediate perceptions and cognitions are true; but 'being' changed, it corroded and died; as this was so, how did 'being' recognize itself and preserve its continuity? Plato introduced the notion of essences as a necessary factor, and with it the proposition that only ideas were eternally and universally true. We can leap ahead at this point and recognize how much Plato contributed to Christian theology when his work became familiar to Augustine in the fourth century.

But we are at the cross to understand the intervention of God in time. Let us be very clear. We are not meditating on the existence of God, which objectively can never be proved. We are meditating on the existence of men seeking self-knowledge of being and whether that can have individual meaning without introducing God. Socrates did not think so, nor did Christ. The problem might be put like this: how were the evangelists to compose a life of God that differed from Socrates' insight of God as infinitely past, or the Judaistic concept of God as related through a covenant to the race?

Perhaps to follow what the evangelists were about it would be easier to understand the massive limitations of both Greek thought and Judaism to provide an alternative to Roman efficiency. The limitations could be expressed like this; Greek society and Greek thought recognized the priority of individual awareness while committing the bulk of the population to slavery; Judaism, in emphasising the priority of the race's relationship in the Covenant, confined the individual experience to prescribed attitudes. What did Christianity offer?

The insights of Christianity provided what Greek thought and Judaism lacked, to the citizens of Rome who most needed it, that is to the poor, the destitute, the under-privileged, the slaves. It provided an awareness of freedom that could be experienced now and projected into the future.

'My God, my God, why hast thou forsaken me?'

Before coming to this central word of freedom let us consider what sort of God would be different from the Jehovah of Judaism and the God whom Socrates extracted and conceived from the collapse of Greek theogony. Suppose as we have suggested from the beginning that all a Christian was required to believe was that 'the eternal truth, God, has come into being in time, has been born like everyone else, has grown up like everyone else, and so on and so forth.' The offence to Judaism in Christianity lay in the central message of the New Testament, that God made Christ the cursed one for us, the revelation of God by way of an individual. The folly of Christianity to the Greeks lay in the paradox that the eternal truth has come into being in time. The paradox existed in Greek thought by way of contradiction, if only to be repudiated by Aristotle, 'the same attribute cannot at the same time belong and not belong to the same subject and in the same respect . . .' This is precisely what the evangelists were about, that at the same time the attributes of God and man came together in the person of Christ. What were the evangelists proposing that Socrates and Aristotle omitted? To Socrates God was the accidental occasion for truth and self-knowledge, a vanishing moment, hidden in eternity so to speak, and so incorporated with it that even if this truth from eternity is sought for it cannot be found, because in an eternal consciousness there is neither here nor there, but only an everywhere and nowhere. To the evangelists the moment in time of the pattern of the life of the New Testament reaching its fulfilment in the cross was decisive; it had such a decisive significance that they were never able to forget it either in time or eternity; indeed the evangelists say that the eternal which up to now did not exist came into existence in this moment.

If a notion of time was at the heart of the Greek rejection of Christianity as a folly where did the offence lie within Judaism?

Suppose for a moment, although it is impossible to suppose it, suppose that Christianity had not happened. Suppose that the Jews with their great insights into the movement of a monotheistic deity had continued as they had for centuries, conducting their dialogue with God and the race, each expanding in qualities of grace as the experience of suffering interpenetrated their life and existence. Suppose, and I remind you that it is impossible to suppose it, that the Jews had come to the end of their side of the dialogue and (just suppose; I will not warn you this time! suppose) that it was God's turn to speak. Just suppose! How would He do it? We know from the Old Testament in dialogue with the Jews that Jehovah had evolved from a primitive jealous God to the expression of mercy and compassion. In Micah the anonymous prophet of the south tells us:

'He hath showed thee, O man, what is good;
  and what doth Jehovah require of thee,
But to do justly, and to love mercy,
  and to walk humbly with thy God?'

And now that it is God's turn to speak, how would He do it?

Is it just possible, just infinitely possible, that He might wish to reveal Himself as a man; for one thing is certain—this would be in character with His eternity. As long as the race lasted, He would endure, man would endure; this was the nature of eternity. But how would He do it?

Clearly He could not do it by revealing Himself as the exceptional. To do so would invite idolatrous worship, and the Jews in their growth had disposed of idolatry centuries before Christ.

Might He reveal himself as a King? Possibly, but even that would limit His revelation too much to a specific time and organisation of society. There might come a time when kings, like volcanoes, were extinct. The title could be used ironically, of course; it had been conferred thus on Jesus 'The King of the Jews.'

What indeed if in His infinite wisdom God willed to express Himself in a situation at the furthest extreme from that source of ultimate power and responsibility that human beings continually attributed to Him. There might come a time when the irony of the title was forgotten and men might really look on Him as king, the all-powerful, the most gracious, the first cause, the alpha and omega. There must be a constraint and indirectness in God's revelation of Himself, therefore He cannot freely reveal His hiddenness as any kind of superiority. Suppose He chose to reveal Himself in time, is it not possible that He might do this through a life with such qualities and in such a way that men might be free to recognize Him? As a man? But what kind of man? If not superior, then as a servant?

The Jews had already thought of this, just as the Psalmist had anticipated this word from the cross. Deutero-Isaiah tells us:

> 'Behold, my servant shall prosper,
> he shall be lifted up, exalted to the heights.'

Then in the following chapter (53) he goes on:

> 'He grew up before the Lord like a young plant
>
> whose roots are in parched ground;
> he had no beauty, no majesty to draw our eyes,
> no grace to make us delight in him;
> his form, disfigured, lost all the likeness of a man,
>
> his beauty changed beyond human semblance.
> He was despised, he shrank from the sight of men,
> tormented and humbled by suffering;
>
> We despised him, we held him of no account,

a thing from which men turn their eyes.

Yet on himself he bore our sufferings,
our torments he endured,
while we counted him smitten by God.'

'My God, my God, why hast thou forsaken me?'

Is this how it goes, the servant suffering; the suffering servant? If God is love and desires me to acquire knowledge of myself freely He cannot reveal Himself to me in time as a superior like a king, no, He must be my equal or less, as a servant for my freedom then to recognize Him is total. Nothing stands in the way of our relationship—except my will if I choose not to recognize Him.

Again, if God reveals Himself to me as a servant it must be as a suffering servant, not because Isaiah describes His experience among men so; the physical, psychological sufferings are nothing to Christ. We can be absolutely certain as he assured forgiveness to all, and the thieves that they would be with him in death, that if God is to suffer in His love for us it must be for a reason that is uniquely His, something that separates Him absolutely from mankind.

This Christ knew, that however much God desires to be my equal He knows that by His very nature He cannot be; eternity separates us. This eternity Christ knew, and this difference he suffered. And this suffering is the badge of Christianity, the water mark that stains all transient life and proclaims its corroding humanity. The infinite qualitative difference between God and man.

The task of the evangelists then was so to compose a life of God which would entail no sacrifice of integrity on the part of men. (I say nothing here of the invidious actions of the Church through history, nor of the great service; these have no part in a meditation which is concerned with the individual Christian.) This I can see. I am freely here. But can it be that God as man in time should place Himself at the furthest extremity from God's love? My task, remember, is to understand God's love as the creative impulse towards self-knowledge. So it was for Socrates, so for the Hebrew prophets, so for Christ himself. And yet, there is the Paradox of Christianity—the God in time!

How do I understand this? Is there something in our experience of the world and ourselves today that can make sense of this? Is it like this? Each man in the universe inherits a situation composed of people and objects and nature. Communication between people about people and objects and nature is accepted and possible because of language which can describe and instruments that measure; we call this the objective and external world in which each man participates through his senses and his feelings. But man, the person, differs from objects and nature because by his nature he can reflect on himself. The mind perceives the self as object and reflects; this activity we understand as inwardness or subjectivity.

This activity is always ethical because the initial impulse to reflection arises from a situation in life in which the self, remembering itself, recognizes its failure to live by its own instinctive ethical standards. The normal feelings then in increasing inwardness are of guilt, doubt, and despair, the nothingness of time, place empty of all meaning, and at its most extreme, abandonment by God and loss of identity. This reflection on the self is absolutely personal and totally incommunicable because its occasion is unpredictable and its season is the present. While it lasts the mind is cloistered in stillness, in the silence of the inward self. (Wittgenstein was not a Christian, but did he not describe the problem of the evangelists—which they solved in this cry—when he said, 'But here is the problem, a cry which cannot be called a description, which is more primitive than any description, for all that serves as a description of the inner life.')

Now I understand Mary's silence. A sword must have pierced her heart also and revealed her thoughts whether it was not all a deceit—this that had been predicted for her by the Archangel Gabriel. And in the silence did Mary ask herself the question whether she was humble enough to believe that she was the chosen one, the mother of God?

Let me place myself alone in this position, because this is where each man arrives at some time of life—abandoned by God. This recognition man has by himself, for God cannot be discontinuous. There cannot be one moment when God is alive and the next he dies; eternity will not suffer this, for it would lose its identity.

Mary's silence is the subjective correlative at hearing this word from the cross. She heard it; to us it is only a possibility. Only a possibility—except under one condition. Suppose we call this condition faith? A gift from the man on the cross; we are there by his invitation. What is faith? Faith reverses belief which can be proved objectively; by faith a man's heart is pierced and in following Mary is opened to humility.

Humility is to will one thing, for one thing I see at this moment, this precise moment before the cross; hearing this word is something that transcends reason, something that cannot be explained, something that no-one can grasp but myself, but in so far as I can grasp it it is open to everyone to grasp. Something I freely recognize, as every one is free to recognize, that humility is to will one thing, the understanding that suffering and love are held by the spirit in the inwardness of faith.

'My God, my God, why hast thou forsaken me?'

For in relation to the absolute there is only one tense: the present. For him who is not contemporary with the absolute—for him it has no existence. And as Christ is the absolute, it is easy to see that with respect to Him there is only one situation; that of contemporaneousness. The five, the seven, the fifteen, the eighteen hundred years are neither here nor there: they do not change Him, neither do they in any wise reveal who He was, for who He is is revealed only to Faith.

SØREN KIERKEGAARD

THE SIXTH WORD

Father, into thy hands I commit my spirit.

Luke 23: 46

'BY now it was about midday and a darkness fell over the whole land, which lasted until three in the afternoon; the sun's light failed. And the curtain of the temple was torn in two. Then Jesus gave a loud cry and said, "Father, into thy hands I commit my spirit;" and with these words he died.'

It is Luke who gives us this word, and it is only in Luke that we find it—Luke, the great reconciler of the New Testament. There are the most powerful, overwhelming reasons why in our mosaic of the pattern of the life of the New Testament I place this word here.

For a moment we might be with Mark and Matthew as they describe the scene out of which the previous word sprang—it was then midday, and you will remember it was three in the afternoon when Jesus cried aloud 'Eli, Eli, lema sabachthani', which being translated means 'My God, my God, why hast thou forsaken me?'

What are we to gather from this? Are the evangelists telling a garbled story, are they men so under the charisma of Christ that they can no longer think for themselves, that they are impervious to the coherence and truth of the matters they are recalling.

'My God, my God, why hast thou forsaken me?'
'Father, into thy hands I commit my spirit.'

Let us explore this. After the great central cry there are only two words left, the one we are considering and the final acceptance. So far we have placed these words in a certain order of logic, a logic we are to understand as being concerned with the spirit—the logic of the spirit, but spirit being revealed under and through the most dire physical conditions, by a human being continually in a situation in life having relationships ordinary, neighbourly and intimate. Christianity is spirit, spirit is inwardness.

We have seen our understanding of the spirit grow under the pressure of the situation of the cross, Christ increasing in solitude and the awareness of suffering leading to a new understanding of love as a heart is pierced and open to the grace of humility. Humility is to will one thing—to be there—in silence. Does this movement of inwardness end there? If we were now to say that it is finished, then indeed we could say that inwardness had come to its end, where in every other occasion of life it reaches its destination—what we understand when we talk of hidden inwardness. Christ would have demonstrated what is meant by hidden inward suffering, and we could have gone on to say that God's intervention in the world had been revealing but it had not been creative. We would have been left in a state of infinite sorrow.

'Father, into thy hands I commit my spirit.'

Let me turn away from the cross for a moment. Let us turn to one who has been called the wisest man in the world—Socrates. The teaching of Socrates was understood in a sense which prompted his students to ask questions of themselves. (From the standpoint of the Socratic thought every point of departure in time is by that fact accidental, an occasion, a vanishing moment; the teacher himself is no more than this; and if he offers himself and his instruction on any other basis, he does not give but takes away, and is not even the learner's friend.) When Socrates isolated himself from every human relationship by insisting that his first duty as a human being was to exist, he assumed that everyone must do the same. This view of life is an essential secret because it cannot be communicated directly. The most that Socrates could do was to help another to achieve the same view, and his artistry consisted entirely in his ability to rouse birth pangs of this sort of view. In the Socratic view each individual is his own centre and the entire world centres in him, because his self-knowledge is a knowledge of God.

When Socrates had been tried for corrupting the youth of Athens and sentenced to death, you will remember that, when he drank the hemlock and those standing round might have expected him to curse those who had tried him and condemned him unjustly, all he said was, 'Tell Aesculepius, I owe him a cock.' That is all Plato tells us of the end of Socrates, and in this ending he preserved his inwardness to the end. Against all the expectation of his listeners, Socrates had not surrendered to his emotions; his mind, his spirit, his will, preserved his actions to the end. 'Tell Aesculepius,' he said simply with a serene detachment, 'I owe him a cock.'

One would say that in the death of Socrates the classical Stoic attitude to the world originated; the posture that nobly accepted 'the slings and arrows of outrageous fortune,' triumphing over them by ignoring them. What Socrates, the wisest man in the world, communicated was an attitude. And indeed, if the evangelists had come to the end of their revelation with the words, 'My God, my God, why hast thou forsaken me?' they would have done for Christ precisely what Plato did for Socrates. They would have conveyed an attitude to us, they would have conveyed precisely what the author of the twenty-second Psalm conveys to us in his first words—an attitude of pure despair. For who has not felt lost in the world, deserted, absolutely solitary, with no relief anywhere, that moment when we come face to face with our inability to communicate anything of meaning, let alone value? Bereft of will—of immediate will instantly at our command.

If Christ had stopped with his central word he would have been entirely in the convention of the classical world, but he would have lacked eternity. Instead out of the particularity of his life he reached out to grasp eternity.

'Father, into thy hands I commit my spirit.'

With this word from the cross Christ introduced an entirely new movement in to the communication of life. I can see the nobility of Socrates as an objective fact; with this word of Christ's I must open myself to understand it. And I must understand it in the sense that Paul understood his Christianity, 'Not I, but Christ lives in me.'

We must begin to see how casually, without any apparent awareness, the evangelists come together to reveal in the most secret and persuasive manner the inwardness of Christianity. It is as if Matthew and Mark on the one hand, and Luke on the other, come upon two halves of one truth at the same time. It happens instinctively; without deliberation the evangelists come together, they unite in revealing how Christianity is to be communicated. What Christianity is we know from the Bible; it is God's intervention in history through His relationship with a man. How is this done? By a life—a life, only a life.

It is a movement inwards in the understanding of suffering and love, a movement outwards in commitment first to God, and then to the neighbour, the person next to you—not your choice, but the person placed next to you. The paradigm of life has been expressed. It is as if on that sombre Good Friday at about three in the afternoon, on a hill called Calvary, when the earth was shaking about him, a man called out in his suffering 'My God, my God, why have you forsaken me——' and precisely at the same time in his love could not forbear to cry out 'Father, into thy hands I commit my spirit.'

With that double movement Christ went beyond Socrates. Far from keeping his inwardness to himself, which was something he, like Socrates, was entitled to do, he expressed it to the world for the world to accept or reject. The world was free to do either. That was the point. A man might admire Socrates and preserve his own inwardness. Here on the cross admiration is irrelevant; a man is absorbed inwardly or not at all: absorbed inwardly, with a complete attention outwards—to Christ.

The pattern of two ways of life has been demonstrated: inwards, in suffering and despair; outwards, in humility and love, dedication and commitment. The pattern had been expressed in a situation that was entirely of man's contriving, not God's. The power of its persuasion lay precisely in that the revelation was not accompanied by thunderbolts or any of those tricks which the Greek gods indulged in at the expense of the poor mortals in the war at Troy, as Homer tells us. No, the cross is a symbol of man's power and authority which God took upon Himself to declare the nature of the human heart.

This movement of Christ's, inwards in despair, outwards in love, was no edict from a throne that men were compelled to obey. It was no manifesto issued by a group of politicians bent on changing the world; nothing like the cry 'Workers of the world, unite; you have nothing to lose but your chains!'

This was not the result of the silent brooding by a professor in a university who in a burst of generosity decides to give the world the benefit of his thought. No, this was a life saying something about life, and it was in life that the revelation had to be communicated if men were to live it, and not just think about it and admire it. No, the revelation was made, had to be made at such an extremity from man's natural way of thinking of God as to involve the maximum risk for the observer. Risk? The risk that the observer was listening not merely to the words of God, but God Himself. And so to the faith that holds the observer at the cross is added the essential characteristic of Christian faith—risk.

The movement continues, the spirit breathes because it is a dialogue, a dialogue that moves continually as it passes from the evangelists through the centuries to each individual observer who finds himself at the cross, the unique situation of solitude.

The attitude of Socrates to death might well be emulated, not allowing death one moment of surrender and yet one died. But so to live one's life in hiddenness and then, as death approached, to express as publicly as it could be not merely how death could be sustained, but to go beyond all considerations of death and so to express in this moment what it meant to live—to live in existence—towards another—I and you. (As it were . . . I, in despair, 'My God, my God, why has thou forsaken me?' yet, to you in love 'Father, into thy hands I commit my spirit.')

It seems to me that God trusted His Son to do just this, if men's hearts were to be pierced and held. We can understand the desolation of being forsaken, we can sympathize well enough. What we did not expect in all the world was this cry towards the Father. If there is nothing more in this word, there is evidence that the man on the cross is in command of himself, of his will, but could not we go beyond that and suggest that wherever a man lives a Christian life there is a movement inward as the heart is pierced and we die to the world and at the same moment we are alive as in hope we look outwards? I and Thou.

As we might see it Christ was free to reveal himself like this now because as God He had been placed in a position of complete inaccessibility—by men. Anything more than the complete inaccessibility of God now would be a limitation on man's freedom—man's freedom to choose—to choose to be there. Men chose freely to place God in this situation; God totally bound incites men freely to find themselves there. In the person of Christ we can participate. And just as Christ recognized that to be made whole he had to commit himself in trust, so we before the cross recognize that we are partial creatures through and through and must continually choose by an act of will to look outwards to be made whole.

To his contemporaries Christ could only say, 'I will give myself as a sacrifice for the sins of the world, and for thy sins too.' Is this, then, easier to believe than when He had done it, when He had actually given His life? or is the comfort greater when He says that He will do it than when He has done it? No, not till He has done it, not till then is doubt made impossible as it possibly can be; and only when Christ is offered as the sacrifice of atonement, not till then, is the comfort at hand which makes the doubt of the forgiveness of sins as impossible—yes, as impossible as it possibly can be; for then, it is only for faith that this comfort exists.

SØREN KIERKEGAARD

THE SEVENTH WORD

It is finished.

John 19: 30

'A jar stood there full of sour wine; so they soaked a sponge with the wine, fixed it on a javelin, and held it up to his lips. Having received the wine, he said, "It is accomplished!" He bowed his head and gave up his spirit.'

The mosaic of the Christian revelation of inwardness is almost complete.

Appropriately it is John, and only John, who has this word—John, the theologian of the evangelists, completing the science of God. But again we have the continuity of incident, the overlapping of everyday things out of which we hear the last word, to disentangle it for ourselves.

There is the wine which was present in Mark and Matthew after the central cry of desolation. In Mark 'Then Jesus gave a loud cry and died', in Matthew Jesus 'again gave a loud cry and breathed his last', in Luke 'Then Jesus gave a loud cry and said, "Father, into thy hands I commit my spirit"; and with these words he died.' And now in John 'Having received the wine, he said, "It is accomplished!" He bowed his head and gave up his spirit.' And we, following the movement which began with Christ's triumph over the external world by forgiveness, come to that moment which gives finality to his inwardness. 'It is accomplished.'

Some may prefer this word as it is translated in the Authorized Version. 'It is finished.'

Suffering, love, inwardness, humility, outwards in faith, risk, finality. With these words a man might recognize the direction his life must take if he is to be contemporary with Christ. There is of course the danger that because Christ recognized the finality of his life a man might be tempted to think that he could say the same of his own; and then, having said this, he could proceed to participate in the resurrection as Christ did, which would really show that he had submitted to the temptation, the temptation that he failed to see the difference between those things that pertain to God and those that remain in man's control. The failure to accept finality—the temptation of testing God, the temptation that because of the resurrection Christ did not really mean this word, that for some inexplicable reason the man Christ did not die. The evangelists clearly believed that he died, for this is the one fact in the situation that they all agree on, that they all report. And we would think that the evangelists, having composed the life would have left it there to speak for itself, as it did to Paul. For the beginning of Christianity in a sense can be found in that moment on the Damascus road, when the man Saul became aware of the new way of Christianity and in the penetrating situation of the cross could ask himself of the man Jesus, 'Saul, Saul, why do you persecute me?'; forever after this Paul would claim 'Not I, but Christ lives in me.' And this was before the Gospels were composed. (We cannot at this time measure the weight of oral tradition in early Christianity. If we assume, as I have done here, that the Letters of Paul precede the composition of the Gospels then Paul's first move towards Christianity, as recounted by Luke in Acts 9, becomes enormously significant as the first evidence as to how Christianity works. The question is not so much what Luke described on the Damascus road but, Christianity being what it is, how could he have done it otherwise?)

Let us consider for a moment what the evangelists were doing in the resurrection literature. For clearly, as they are all so sure in their various ways that Christ died, why the resurrection?—why the anxiety at the tomb?

The disciples, unlike Mary, were not present at the crucifixion so far as we are told. They had all fled after the arrest in the garden, except Peter, who denied him at the trial. The evangelists, knowing that the disciples had not heard the last words from the cross and aware that they had missed the most profound insights of his teaching decided to convey this in the resurrection literature. They were conveying something about a life. And how, we must ask ourselves, could they have done otherwise? Let us consider what they were trying to do.

Luke says (it is Luke again) after Jesus was taken down from the cross and laid in the tomb . . . 'But on the Sunday morning very early they [the women who had accompanied him from Galilee] came to the tomb bringing the spices they had prepared. Finding that the stone had been rolled away from the tomb, they went inside; but the body was not to be found. While they stood utterly at a loss, all of a sudden two men in dazzling garments were at their side. They were terrified, and stood with eyes cast down, but the men said

"Why search among the dead for one who lives? Remember what he told you while he was still in Galilee, about the Son of Man: how he must be given up into the power of sinful men and be crucified, and must rise again on the third day." '

Suppose now at this moment, balanced between the finality of the crucifixion and the resurrection on the third day, we were to remember as we have been doing during this meditation that the revelation of Christianity must be seen as a dialogue and a movement—a dialogue between Christ and the evangelists, as they compose the life of the hidden God, a movement because in nature and history there is no finality. If we are to understand the living revelation of God in Christ the last place we must search for it is among the dead, and yet it is revealed by one who said 'It is finished.' At its most naïve the women's search might lead to the erection of a few idols, images of one lying as it were dead, but it would not be a revelation of that spirit which is inwardness. What the resurrection is concerned with, is: how are we to know and recognize a life that is eternal? Must we like Thomas want to touch the wounds before being assured of their reality? Does that assure us of anything more than that they are wounds, visible to a contemporary, but hidden from the generations that come after? Even if we in a moment of fantasy could do that, would this be an understanding of that spirit which is inwardness? Thomas standing before the risen Christ can say 'My Lord and my God!' But where was the risk in Thomas's faith?

Again, must we, like the two disciples on the road to Emmaus, have recalled to us the story of God's revelation of Himself from Moses right down through

Jewish history before recognizing the leap that was made in Christianity—the human intervention of God in time? It is possible that we might be like the two on the road to Emmaus and fail to recognize the mode of God's intervention—that is, that it was in spirit, in inwardness. Indeed, we might be assured in some sense through the appearances of Christ in the resurrection that there is a God, and our grounds would be just as superstitious as the 'evidence' that the astronaut brought back from his voyage in space to announce 'There is no God!' Both are superstitious in their understanding of the nature of Christianity, which is a communication about life, not ideas, thoughts, abstractions and dreams.

If Christ is revealing the inwardness of God, the evangelists are trying to tell us something about how we may understand eternity, that eternity can be of interest only to God, and that Christianity is the only reasonable way by which a life can interpenetrate eternity; that this cannot be done by the body (though the body has a life), but only by spirit, that spirit which is inwardness.

Just as at one and the same moment Christ cried out in his desolation 'My God, my God, why hast thou forsaken me?' together with that cry of grace 'Father, into thy hands I commit my spirit,' so the evangelists are trying to tell us that we must hold the crucifixion and the resurrection together in our understanding.

Remember Mary; Mary to whom so much was promised, and who at the cross suffered, Mary in her humility believed, she was silent. This seems to be Christ's answer whenever the matter of God's eternity is raised, for in all the resurrection literature Christ does not appear to his mother. He did not need to. He trusted her. In the face of his experience of the world (he had been totally forsaken) that was a great risk. Yet she continued in humility to believe, for she was silent. Christ trusted Mary and she was silent.

Christ trusted. The demand of life is that we must live and trust. Socrates lived and trusted, and he found Plato. Christ lived and first trusted his mother, whose heart was pierced. Let us turn to Luke, the great reconciler; for it is Luke who first tells us that Mary's heart will be pierced.

Fifty days after the resurrection Luke tells us in Acts that the disciples were in Jerusalem—'While the day of Pentecost was running its course they were all together in one place, when suddenly there came from the sky a noise like that of a strong driving wind, which filled the whole house where they were sitting.' How can Luke tell us otherwise of the Holy Spirit, of His universality and how all who were crowded there heard their own language spoken, of its nature when Peter spoke? He talked of the man Jesus, of his crucifixion and resurrection, of how it should be received 'when they heard this, they were pierced to the heart.' From the piercing of Mary's heart at the presentation of the child Jesus in the Temple, to the Lord through his life and crucifixion, to the piercing of the hearts at Pentecost the pattern of the inwardness that is Christianity had been completed by Luke the great reconciler.

And so Good Friday and Easter Day come together. We are still to understand the finality of the last word. 'It is finished.'

It is to life we turn, to the precise life which, as John says, 'speaks the truth so that you too may believe' and again 'They shall look on him whom they pierced.' What life? What sort of life that is not merely at one with the species, but rises above it? The pattern has been raised before us, on a cross; we have been given an example.

It is a life that begins in forgiveness and in suffering acquires a new self-awareness.

It is a life which views the world steadily and respects the truth of each single person.

It is a life grounded in freedom and recognizes that where freedom is expressed suffering is inevitable.

It is a life that in suffering is mediated by love, for as God is eternal, love is eternal, and as the eternal cannot change, love is continually open to all. To all—*to all;* there is no exclusiveness in love.

But then comes the revelation. Before a man understands the 'all' he must understand himself, himself in inwardness. And in this sense the individual, the subject, the person, while a part of the race, a part of the species, is also above the species, above the race, because through Christ he participates in eternity, because now he understands spirit.

There is no sense in which the individual spirit can be generalized, because there is no sense in which we can generalize the fifth word of the cross, 'My God, my God, why hast thou forsaken me?', and so there is no general sense by which the individual heart is pierced.

Then the miracle of Christianity, the moment the heart is pierced, it is open to a concern for life—to others. In that moment death is abolished, for we have been released from our bodies. If this is the pattern of the Christian life we are each of us individually in the position to say 'It is finished.'

Very well, you may say, it *is* finished; and, as an

observer at the cross, you might concur with the evangelists that, Christ having said the words, and particularly that last word, it was all over, and it was a sad story. And if it was not all over, following the pattern of centuries you might with millions of others go on to rejoice in the glory of Easter Day which proclaims the eternity of God. And perhaps you might in a very human way wish to participate in that eternity.

But this is not why you are present at the cross on Good Friday; to gain a unique insight into eternity. No, not that, but it is just possible that at the back of your mind there was an invitation from one who had said to you 'Come unto me all you that travail and are heavy laden and I will refresh you.'

That is why on each Good Friday we are here. We are not forced to be here, but of our own free will. Freely we have come here, for this is the ground of the situation of the cross. Because freedom is the ground, we are free to choose. Just as Christ in freedom did absolutely the inevitable so we inevitably are free to choose to be at the cross. There is no other way.

If now there is some way by which the individual can add to his partial understanding of himself, some dimension by which he can achieve a wholeness so that he can truly say 'I and Thou', how does he manifest this newfound wholeness to the world? What is the temper of this 'whole' life? What is there that the observer catches in reflection from the pattern? The pattern of the hidden God.

There is in the evangelists' revelation of the life of Christ in the New Testament a wonderful unity of character in action. Everything that Christ says is not merely inevitable but necessary. And what is necessary to make the inevitability of the life on the cross not only humanly bearable but humanly communicable? Just as Christ has invited us to be with him at the cross so he has assured us in the most absolute terms that whatever situation he is in he will overcome it. We have his assurance of this. Did he not tell us, 'For my yoke is easy, and my burden is light.' This yoke easy? This burden light?

Easy and light in God's sense, not ours. Easy in the sense that the beauty of the firmament and the grace of truth is easy because it is now finished; it was something accomplished in eternity but continually wonderful in our eyes; light in the sense that otherwise the cross would become a burden and earthbound; without buoyancy, it would lack spirit.

The buoyancy of the cross, and through it Christianity, is the characteristic which the Christian must always have in heart and mind when he faces the world. The measure of his success in the practice of Christianity will be the degree to which his life will go unnoticed—as Christ's went unnoticed. The hidden God will then be revealed in life towards another life in wholeness. There is rejoicing where beauty is seen. But it is in a man's life that eternity is seen as he chooses Christ as the pattern.

The world as it turns through the passing centuries reveals itself in suffering. Christianity will have nothing to do with a world in which suffering is not present, because freedom will not be present. Freedom in our century is one of the prevailing winds. The other is equality, and all are equal before God. Wherever we turn in our tormented world the longing to be free with equality expresses itself in suffering.

To this world of ours the cross is continually

present as the pattern through which the longing and the suffering can be reconciled in the reality of God's love as lived in the pattern of the cross. The test of a great poet is not what he says but what he does to us, the vision he presents to us which transforms us. How much greater is this vision, the vision of absolute reality, the thing itself, in which a man might find something more than a vision—he might find unity and peace. He might even find himself contemporary with Christ, and be moved as the centurion was moved to say 'Truly this man was a son of God.'

But then he dies. And His death alters everything infinitely. Not that his death abolished the fact that at the same time He is the Pattern; no, but His death becomes the infinite guarantee with which the striver starts out, the assurance that infinite satisfaction has been made, that to the doubtful and disheartened there is tendered the strongest pledge—impossible to find anything more reliable!—that Christ died to save him, that Christ's death is the atonement and satisfaction.

SØREN KIERKEGAARD